Stories from Kindergarten

and the Word of God

Tana Hoff

STORIES FROM KINDERGARTEN
AND THE WORD OF GOD
Copyright © 2020 by Tana Hoff

Unless otherwise noted, all Scripture quotations are taken from the Holy Bible, New Living Translation (NLT), copyright ©1996, 2004, 2007 by Tyndale House Foundation. Used by permission of Tyndale House Publishers, Inc., Carol Stream, Illinois 60188. All rights reserved.

Print ISBN: 978-1-4866-2037-1
eBook ISBN: 978-1-4866-2038-8

Word Alive Press
119 De Baets Street, Winnipeg, MB R2J 3R9
www.wordalivepress.ca

WORD ALIVE
—P R E S S—

Cataloguing in Publication may be obtained through Library and Archives Canada

This book is dedicated to my mother, Jeanette Kozack, who served her church community with love and dedication. She was my listening ear for many of the stories in this book right up until she went to be with the Lord in 2014.

Contents

Prophetic Word

"I inquired of the Lord about you, Tana, and this is what I sensed from Him. 'She is My precious, precious daughter. She works hard and she puts her whole heart, being, and creativity into what she does. She truly knows how to love and serve. She gives from the heart and her motives are pure. She has no guile in her. I love when she spends time with Me. I look forward to those times. In fact, I treasure those moments with Tana. She does well. Her worship means everything to Me. I love how she uses her gifts to honour and love Me.'"

—Joyce Howard
colleague, August 2019

About the Front-Cover Picture

Music was one of the main ingredients in my kindergarten program. The day always started with songs that welcomed the students and provided a joyful, uplifting, comfortable, and inviting environment—the perfect inclusion activity!

As I strummed away on the guitar, the students sang along to tunes that helped them learn classmates' names, the alphabet, days of the week, rhymes, classroom rules and routines, and more. Often, students would pretend to strum on their own guitar as we sang by watching and copying my actions.

We sang throughout the day to prepare for recess and lunch. We sang about what we were learning. We sang the students' favourite songs; student requests were common. I quickly learned that caution was needed with requests, as some of the lyrics of the popular songs their older siblings were listening to might not have been appropriate for little ears. This was of no concern to the kindergarten kids; they uninhibitedly belted out the lyrics word for word, unaware of the meaning behind them. And at the end of the day, we always sang the goodbye song.

How This Book Came to Light

Stories from Kindergarten and the Word of God is a collection of incidents and experiences that transpired over my thirty-year teaching career. Twenty-seven of those years were spent teaching in public schools and the final three years in a private Christian school.

Chronicles are presented in a random order. The short stories are honest, humorous, heartfelt, precious, unique, and genuine. I honestly didn't realize the value of what God was teaching me through these everyday events at the time. Most situations caught me by surprise and had me thinking on my feet.

Upon coming home from an exhausting—yet fulfilling—day of teaching young children, I would recount the events of the day, first to myself, then to my husband when he came home from work, then to my mother through a phone call.

"Mom, I have a story from kindergarten for you today," I'd tell her.

This brought us both laughter, joy, and sometimes tears, depending on the nature of the story.

I pray that these same stories will inspire and uplift you.

Each chapter begins with a question and an idiosyncratic story title to capture your attention and curiosity. The question and title are knit into the heart of the story. Bible verses are provided after each individual story to support the message.

God is working in our everyday life, even if we don't see how this is playing out. Teachers cross the paths of many students throughout their teaching career. I believe God has a divine plan for every single encounter.

Introduction

As I sit and look out the windows of the loft level of my cottage, I see white-capping waves rolling into the shore. The main-level doors are open, allowing the soothing sound of the waves to move through the screen and rise up to my desk and writing space.

It's early morning. The air smells of lilacs and morning dew; other times, the odour of manure from the farm across the lake wafts over when the direction of the wind guides the air toward the southwest side of the lake.

I am now six months into my retirement from my career as an educator of more than thirty years.

A smile of contentment, satisfaction, and nostalgia crosses my face as I think back to the many unique experiences of which I've been blessed to be a part.

What triggers memories?

For example, when you walk into a school building, the first thing with which you're confronted is the smell. The odour is a combination of books, sneakers, perhaps various foods, and definitely freshly mopped floors with a mix of sand, dirt, dust, and sweat hovering in the air above.

It was my first year teaching at one of the Christian schools in the city. I'm remembering the time I accidently walked the pastor's young nephew, who was in my kindergarten class, into the middle post of a double doorframe. With twenty-seven teaching years under my belt, I should've remembered that students do this quite frequently on their own. They certainly don't need guidance from the teacher. We were studying and learning about the senses.

Today's walk through the school building was a planned lesson on properly guiding the visually impaired. Students were partnered together. One student wore a blindfold; the other was the human guide. We had an odd number of students in the class, so I partnered up with one of the students. I was the guide. I had a planned route through various rooms and hallways of the school.

I was focused on walking and talking, ensuring all the students were following along and working hard as guides to their blindfolded friends when *thunk!* My blindfolded student partner walked smack into the middle of a doorpost!

Silence from everybody. One little girl covered her mouth with her hand, her eyes revealed a twinkling expression of humour.

"Are you okay?" I quickly asked the young boy.

He nodded slowly, quite startled at what had just happened.

I apologized.

Fortunately, there was no goose egg or mark on his forehead. The next thing I heard was the little girl giggling. I must admit, I chuckle about it now. There's an old saying, "Do as I say, not as I do" (John Selden, English jurist, legal antiquary, and scholar of Jewish law). These words certainly fit this situation. The sights, sounds, and smells of school linger in my memory to this day.

"How was your day?" my colleagues would frequently ask me.

"Never a dull moment!" I'd always reply.

I would love to share some of these memorable, never-a-dull-moments with you.

What Are Listening Ears?

A visual auditory cue I often used and taught my kindergarten students right at the start of the school year was to "turn on their listening ears." We turned our fingers back and forth beside our ears, like a radio dial, and made a static noise with our mouths.

Along with this action, I would repeat the phrase, "Do your best work." They begin to comprehend that this required focused attention and concentration for an extended period of time—for example, a new concept or skill or activity would be introduced, allowing for observation of student learning by the teacher. It was critical that the students were paying attention and were ready to engage.

One afternoon, while teaching my students, a little girl blurted out unexpectedly, and very adamantly, "Mrs. Hoff, I'm turning *off* my listening ears!"

I can't exactly remember my reply, though my usual response to any student who appeared distracted or otherwise was, "You need to listen"—plain and simple.

This little girl's outburst struck me as amusing for a moment. More importantly, it indicated to me that she was overwhelmed. It was a clear signal that this student was about to tune out.

The Bible has a lot to say about listening and its importance. We need to always keep our ears open to what God is asking us to do—even if we feel overwhelmed.

Tune your ears to wisdom, and concentrate on understanding.
—Proverbs 2:2

Ears to hear and eyes to see—both are gifts from the Lord.
—Proverbs 20:12

Pay close attention to what you hear. The closer you listen, the more understanding you will be given—and you will receive even more.

—Mark 4:24

Story Two: For the Love of Learning

What Does God Reveal About Learning in the Bible?

Making learning exciting and engaging students in the learning process in kindergarten often involves creating something.

Our class was learning about numbers—specifically, the number eight. We made a pair of reading glasses out of construction paper, representing the number eight. After creating the brightly coloured glasses, we participated in a variety of activities to reinforce the number. The students were on task, soaking up the knowledge like sponges. They were quite disappointed when it was time to put their glasses away and get ready for the afternoon recess. I enthusiastically reassured them that they could take their reading glasses home at the end of the day and teach their parents all about the number eight. This seemed to satisfy them.

The next day, I had a morning meeting with a team of colleagues. The grade eight teacher was assigned to cover my class from 9 a.m. to 9:30 a.m. Interesting coincidence.

The teacher was very tall and might've looked like a giant to the kindergarteners, and I'm sure the students looked like munchkins to him, as he was used to teaching the oldest students in the school. Perhaps they all felt a bit intimidated. Their facial expressions were looks of curiosity and puzzlement, perhaps a bit of uneasiness.

After giving a few instructions, I left the classroom to go to my meeting.

"You'll have fun!" I assured them.

Every morning, our class engaged in reading a morning message to start the day. On this particular day, the morning message asked the question, "What did you do with your reading glasses at home?"

I returned to the classroom after my meeting. I was delighted and thrilled to observe the students and the teacher enjoying this time together. They were smiling, laughing, and thoroughly engaged in the discussion.

Before the teacher left the classroom, he shared with me one particular response a student gave when asked what he did with the number eight glasses: "I slept with them!" My colleague told me he couldn't believe the enthusiasm for learning the students expressed. He offered to cover my class anytime.

Keep putting into practice all you learned and received from me—everything you heard from me and saw me doing. Then the God of peace will be with you.

—Philippians 4:9

Story Three: Above the Clouds

Did You See God?

It was nearing spring break. In just a couple of days, I would be off on a much-needed vacation.

My flight was scheduled to leave a day before school was dismissed. A familiar guest teacher would oversee the class. My lessons were well planned for the duration of my absence as well as upon my return to school after the break. Everything was in good order. However, I did not say anything about my absence to my students. From experience, I thought this best, as young students often have many questions and concerns.

Spring break seemed to fly by. The students returned to school with many stories to share with me and each other. One could say they were "sky high" with excitement. The students took turns sharing their experiences.

One little boy spoke up and said, "Where were you? You missed our party!"

I ended our group discussion with my travel journey story. I explained that I travelled far away and needed to ride in an airplane to get to my destination. I continued by saying that the airplane soared up high into the sky and that the houses and buildings looked very tiny; the farmers' fields looked like checker boards; and the lakes looked like miniature shapes. Then the airplane took us "above the clouds." The speed of the airplane and sudden surge higher was thrilling!

I looked at my students sitting so quietly, their little faces intently looking at me. I noticed that the same little boy who had asked where I had been had a serious expression on his face; his eyes were as big as saucers, his gaze intense.

I asked him if he had a question or something to say.

After a moment, he looked up and asked, "Did you see God?"

"Not with my eyes."

I think he was expecting me to say yes! Later that day, I called his mom to tell her the story.

"It sounds like he is paying attention in Sunday school!" she said.

No one has ever seen God. But the unique One, who is himself God, is near to the Father's heart. He has revealed God to us.
—John 1:18

But you may not look directly at my face, for no one may see me and live.

—Exodus 33:20

No one has ever seen God. But if we love each other, God lives in us, and his love is brought to full expression in us.
—1 John 4:12

Story Four: Fishy Heaven

Do Pets Go to Heaven?

Science is one of my favourite subjects! It's an area of study that allows for observation and hands-on learning and a fantastic way to allow for classroom pets. Throughout my career, I've introduced a variety of little creatures in the classroom for my students to learn about: hermit crabs, frogs, aquariums full of different species of fish, and more!

The students designated as VIPs (Very Important People, or leaders for the day) had special duties caring for our classroom pets. We discussed how to carefully and properly feed, clean, and care for our pet friends. I modelled correct methods of handling these small creatures as well as how to use equipment needed to house and keep the critters safe, such as properly closing the lids of pet tanks.

One day, I noticed a little goldfish floating in the class aquarium—not good. We always counted the fish, so I knew the students would realize one would be missing if I disposed of it right then. I decided to wait until lunch recess after the students had eaten and were outside playing. It would also give me time to think about how I would explain what happened to one of our fishy friends.

As soon as the students were all out of the classroom dismissed for recess, I immediately went to rid the aquarium of the floating fish. I couldn't locate the fish net, so I headed to the staffroom to ask the grade two teacher if I could borrow her net. She kindly offered to scoop the fish out of the tank for me and flush the fish away in the kindergarten classroom washroom, located just two feet away from the counter where the aquarium was located.

I became busy talking with my colleagues in the staffroom. The bell rang, signalling the students to return to class. I remembered that I had forgotten to explain to the grade two teacher that she needed to hold the flush handle down for the duration of the flush or the contents in the toilet would not completely be disposed of.

I returned to the classroom and twelve of my students were sitting at the tables, putting on their indoor shoes. I waited by the classroom door for the remaining students. I decided to slip out to the lockers to check on the "doddlers." A moment later, I returned. All the students who were sitting at the tables were gone!

I heard gasps coming from the washroom in our classroom. Hunched and peeking over the toilet were twelve little people pointing at the little fish floating in the toilet. One student commented that someone must have left the aquarium lid open and that the little fish jumped out and landed in the toilet. I stepped in and told them that the fish was not alive anymore. I then flushed the toilet and told the students that he was on his way to "fishy heaven."

One little boy asked if this was the same heaven that people go to.

"No, when we are done here on earth, we are not flushed down the toilet," I replied, spur of the moment.

For the life of every living thing is in his hand, and the breath of every human being.

—Job 12:10

What Is a Gift of the Heart?

I'm thankful God gave me the wisdom to respond lovingly and in a meaningful way for this particular story.

December had always been an upbeat and festive month in the kindergarten class. The final day before the traditional holiday break was celebrated with a Christmas party. I would request that, in lieu of purchasing gifts for me, students could together present a gift to charity in our class's name. We could use this celebrated holiday with its customary gift giving to bless someone in need. Parents were always very receptive to this suggestion.

However, the children insisted on giving their teacher a present. They were always so thrilled to give me their special gift at Christmas. So, we usually ended up doing both.

One by one, I opened the precious gifts, all carefully and beautifully wrapped. The students' faces were bright and happy, their voices ooh-ing and aw-ing at all the nifty gifts.

One little girl was sitting near me. Her long, thick, beautiful golden hair was held neatly together in a ponytail with a hairband. She sat quietly with the most downcast eyes. I knew her family was going through a tough time. At the end of opening gifts, this little girl held out her hand to me. It was crunched up in a fist. I noticed that her golden hair was bouncing around her face and shoulders. As she opened her fist, her ponytail band dropped into the palm of my hand.

"I didn't have time to wrap this," she said quietly. Her eyes changed from disheartened to uncertainty.

"Oh my! I can't believe it! How did you know that this is just what I needed?" I responded enthusiastically. "When I play hockey, my long hair falls into my eyes. Now, I have a very special ponytail band to use!"

This little girl's face brightened, her smile reaching ear to ear. She didn't realize that she blessed me with two gifts that day.

You should remember the words of the Lord Jesus: "It is more blessed to give than to receive."

—Acts 20:35

Story Six: Recess Bell

What Is God's Timing?

It was a beautiful, sunny spring afternoon. The hallways and classrooms were silent. The students were outside enjoying recess. I was soaking up the peace at my desk.

The recess bell rang. The students all piled in, taking off their jackets and joining classmates on the carpet at the listening area. I greeted the students at the classroom door, asking how their recess was.

A very vibrant and apparently perturbed little girl marched in, waving her arms in the air, declaring, "Mrs. Hoff made the bell ring and we all had to come in!"

"Honey, if it were up to me, you would still be out there for another twenty minutes!"

I said this not because it was a wonderfully nice day, offering beautiful weather for the students to enjoy the great outdoors. Rather, I said this because I was truly enjoying the serenity of an unoccupied, tranquil classroom.

The clock had struck 2:30 p.m.; the bell rang. The students returned to their classrooms. The students had no control over this. I personally didn't have any authority to extend recess.

Most likely, each one of us can identify with wanting or waiting for something, such as an extended recess break, and wanting it immediately. It can be difficult displaying patience, especially if we don't have control over the situation.

Waiting for God to answer prayers often requires endurance with great fortitude. But we know His timing is perfect.

> *Wait patiently for the Lord. Be brave and courageous. Yes, wait patiently for the Lord.*
>
> —Psalm 27:14

> *For everything there is a season, a time for every activity under heaven.*
>
> —Ecclesiastes 3:1

How Do We Perceive the World Around Us?

Life's issues or situations can sometimes be seen as larger than they are. It's a matter of perspective.

Perspective is important. The decisions we make and how we live our lives are usually based on how we view things.

Gym class often occurred outdoors. With more than five hundred students sharing the one indoor gymnasium space, alternative environments were often used.

My favourite alternative space was the school playground. The students and staff were very blessed to have a large, spacious area with plenty of play structures, sports areas, and a large hill. We made our way out to the playground. The empty structures and vastness of the space were extremely inviting. The students were to follow me to a paved area, where we would all participate in a cooperative game. Then, I would allow for ten minutes of free play before heading back indoors. The plan of action or protocol was routine for our outdoor physical education classes.

Recess dismissal, however, tended to have its own rather chaotic order of getting to one's choice of play. As soon as the students exited the building, they bolted to their destination, usually screaming at the top of their lungs. They looked and sounded like chickens flying the coop to escape a predator!

I was always impressed with my students' display of self-control as we walked over to the space where we would occupy and engage in our group activity. It was so tempting for them to just run off and go in the direction that caught their attention.

But one day, it was not long before I heard a little voice behind me calling out, "Mrs. Hoff, Mrs. Hoff, Mya's on the mountain!"

I immediately looked up at the oversized hill situated among a variety of climbing structures not too far from where we were stationed.

What struck me most was not that this little person was tattling on another student who wasn't following my instructions, but on her own perspective of the size of the hill. It looked like a mountain to this little person.

I winked and replied, "Everybody, let's run and meet Mya on the mountain!" Off we all ran to go play on the "mountain."

> *"My thoughts are nothing like your thoughts," says the Lord. "And my ways are far beyond anything you could imagine. For just as the heavens are higher than the earth, so my ways are higher than your ways and my thoughts higher than your thoughts."*
>
> —Isaiah 55:8–9

Story Eight: Green House

Where Does Food Come From?

Our class was learning about nutrition, studying food groups, learning how to make healthy food choices, and learning where food comes from and grows.

One day, we were learning about fruits and vegetables. As always, class discussions provided a wealth of information. The question-and-answer format worked well, both as a group and individuals, as it gave all students an opportunity to speak. An example of a group response would be: "Nod and say 'yummy' if an apple is a fruit." Individual responses required students to offer their own unique ideas.

I asked the students to raise their hands if they could name a fruit or vegetable, or tell me something about them. Many eager little hands shot up into the air.

"My grandma grows bananas," shared one little girl.

I thought about her declaration for a few seconds in my head (Bananas need a warm climate in which to grow. Could they possibly grow here in the Prairies? Or, does her grandmother live in a warmer country?)

"Does your grandma have a greenhouse?" I finally asked.

"No, she lives in a white house."

Then God said, "Look! I have given you every seed-bearing plant throughout the earth and all the fruit trees for your food.
—Genesis 1:29

Are We Missing Something?

My kindergarten classroom was equipped with its own washroom, the sink and toilet both little people-sized! What a fortunate and appreciated blessing. However, there were a few times when having a washroom in the classroom provided for unique but solvable dilemmas.

One such incident occurred after lunch. While preparing to read a story to the class, I sat in my rocking chair with all the students sitting on the carpet in crisscross-apple-sauce formation. (legs crossed and hands folded in their laps)—all except one student, who was in the washroom sitting on the toilet, legs dangling.

The washroom door was wide open.

"Please close the door," I said to him.

"I don't wanna miss anything!"

"We'll wait for you."

While waiting for our friend, the class and I could easily spend a few minutes chatting about the activities and happenings from over the recess.

The next few words that came from this little boy threw me for a loop, but they also left a smile on my face for the rest of the day.

"You got a magazine?"

We might need to extend our group discussion longer than first thought, I said to myself.

This made me think about how young students don't want to miss a single beat. They're reluctant to settle for anything less than what they're entitled to, or what's being offered to them. They insist on attending school when they're ill for fear of missing something. Thankfully, parents keep them home, even after many pleas and tears by their child that they feel just fine.

They also aren't fond of leaving the classroom to receive extra help with speech or academics—unless they're deemed to be special helpers, doing jobs that couldn't be accomplished without their assistance.

The washroom incident attests to the fact that children simply refuse to miss any part of the story the teacher is reading!

Somewhere along the line as we grow older, this fierce determination to receive everything prepared or planned for us fades. We begin to settle for less. What does God say about missing out? How do we receive everything God has for us?

Keep on asking, and you will receive what you ask for. Keep on seeking, and you will find. Keep on knocking, and the door will be opened to you. For everyone who asks, receives.

Everyone who seeks, finds. And to everyone who knocks, the door will be opened.

—Matthew 7:7–8

Story Ten: Occupied

Can Curiosity Be Harmful?

W e've all heard the expression "curiosity killed the cat." Curiosity can indeed lead you down a dangerous path!

It's easy to fall into sin. For example, you might wonder, "Why is everybody drinking that new sports energy drink? I'll try one and find out." Or maybe, "Those other kids at my high school sure make vaping look inviting. I wonder how it makes you feel!"

Christians need to be careful to walk by the Holy Spirit. We must listen to the inner voice that confirms right over wrong.

The following story is mild; however, it does stress my point. The washroom my class used had a toilet that wasn't flushing properly. The door lock was also broken and students often forgot to knock and unintentionally walked in on one another.

To solve the issue, I made a sign that said "Occupied"— similar to the signs you see on airplane washrooms, except the sign I made was attached to a string in order to hang from the knob. If the students needed to use the washroom, they were to hang the sign before entering. When the students were finished their business, they were to remove the sign and hang it on a hook outside the bathroom door.

One day, the classroom was abuzz with students working and playing at the centres. The noise level wasn't that high, but suddenly, the room fell oddly quiet. I looked up from where I was working with a few students, and there, standing in a long line, were about fourteen students, all noticeably quiet, waiting for their turn to use the washroom.

Now, I'm certain they didn't all have to use the washroom right then and there, but everybody appeared to want to try out the new "Occupied" sign. I didn't say anything; I merely watched with amusement.

I can't tell you whether using the washroom with the sign was any more exciting than without it, but I can tell you this: the students' curiosity mentality was at its finest!

The temptations in your life are no different from what others experience. And God is faithful. He will not allow the temptation to be more than you can stand. When you are tempted, he will show you a way out so that you can endure.

—1 Corinthians 10:13

"Keep watch and pray, so that you will not give in to temptation. For the spirit is willing, but the body is weak!"

—Matthew 26:41

Story Eleven: Jak

How Do We Love One Another?

Jak (name changed) is a little boy whom I taught in kindergarten and Grade One. He was attached to my hip for as long as we were both at school. At the end of September of his kindergarten year, his family went home to the Middle East for a month. They returned at the end of October, but without his mom.

One endearing quality about five-year-old boys is that they love their mothers uniquely. They often express that they want to marry her, until they enter kindergarten, then it's a bit of a toss up between the teacher and the mom. It's cute, but it also displays a strong bond between mother and child.

This was true of Jak and the deep love and affection he showed toward his mother at the start of the school year, and heartache he experienced at being unexpectedly separated from her.

As time went on, Jak and I had many heartfelt talks. Sometimes he would stay in at recess and help me with little jobs around the classroom. Sometimes we would have some hot chocolate. Sometimes I would bring him a special lunch or treat. But mostly, there were just plenty of hugs throughout the school day.

One day, while preparing a science activity over the recess break, Jak blurted out, "My dad says Christians and Muslims dislike each other!"

I looked at this little boy—his round face, big brown eyes looking back at me for perhaps confirmation, comfort, or affirmation.

"Well, Jak, I'm Christian, and I love you; you're Muslim, and you love me."

After that, whenever Jak saw me, even from a distance, his five-year-old voice would bellow down the hallway. "I love you, Mrs. Hoff!"

"I love you too, Jak!"

The following year, along with teaching kindergarten, I was assigned to teach arts education to the Grade One class. Jak and I had continued our close and trusting relationship. One day, we had just finished up with music class with a sing-along. The students requested their favourite songs, singing their hearts out while I accompanied them on the guitar. They left the class for recess, humming the last tune we had sung.

I noticed that Jak hung back. He came up close to me and, out of the blue, pointed at my cross neckless around my neck.

"Mrs. Hoff, if Christians have the cross, what do Muslims have?" he asked me, both seriously and sincerely.

I find I always get these questions when I'm not expecting them!

"I don't know, Jak," I answered honestly. "You will have to ask your dad." With that, I gave him a hug, and off he went to join his friends on the playground.

Sometimes it's best to say nothing at all.

Do all that you can to live in peace with everyone.
—Romans 12:18

"So now I am giving you a new commandment: Love each other. Just as I have loved you, you should love each other."
—John 13:34

Story Twelve: Staffroom Classroom

Where Is Our Permanent Home?

It was mid-October; the weather was cool.

It was a special day; grandparents were filling the school for a celebration in their honour. Every classroom and extra spaces available were full. Scheduled times were allocated for different grade levels to host their grandparents so as not to break the school fire code regulations. The kindergarten grandparents' visit was set for later in the day, so we went about our morning routines.

A knock at our classroom door suddenly changed where we would spend the morning. The maintenance team decided to fix a broken window in our classroom. We needed to relocate to another free space in the school building. The only room available was the staffroom. Off we went.

Once we were settled in, one of my students asked, "Is this your house?"

Understandably, the presence of a fridge, stove, microwave, table, chairs, couches, etc., made this space look like a home. On an off note, I spent so much time at school that it did feel like I lived there. However, I explained that the room we were occupying was a room for the staff to eat lunch and visit with each other.

We are reminded in the Bible that the space and time on this earth we presently occupy is merely temporary. It may have comforts of sorts, but it is not permanent for those who choose Christ.

One day, suddenly, we will be caught up with the Lord to spend eternity in our true forever home, with God Himself.

For the Lord himself will come down from heaven with a commanding shout, with the voice of the archangel, and with the trumpet call of God. First, the believers who have died will rise from their graves. Then, together with them, we who are still alive and remain on the earth will be caught up in the clouds to meet the Lord in the air. Then we will be with the Lord forever.

—1Thessalonians 4:16–17

"There is more than enough room in my Father's home. If this were not so, would I have told you that I am going to prepare a place for you? When everything is ready, I will come and get you, so that you will always be with me where I am."

—John 14:2–3

"However, no one knows the day or the hour when these things will happen, not even the angels in heaven or the Son himself. Only the Father knows."

—Mark 13:32

Story Thirteen: Boots!

Are We Ready?

Getting ready for recess during the winter or spring seasons can be a challenging task for many kindergartners. I would always sing a little song as we got dressed. The song helped the children remember the most efficient order in which to put on each clothing item. Boots or outdoor shoes were always the final item.

Being prepared for the weather with proper clothing is essential for a fun and safe recess break outside.

The students' boots were kept on a boot shelf in the boot room area located down the hall from the classroom. The children would grab them off the shelf, put them on, and then line up at the door to the playground. I was always on hand to help with any issues, such as ensuring the right boot was on the right foot, pulling those snow pants over the boots to prevent snow from getting in the boot, straightening out boot liners that were disformed from sweaty little feet from the constant putting on and pulling off of the boot, etc.

As the students stood in line one day waiting for the bell to ring, I heard "my" voice through one of the little girls in our class. It put a smile on my face.

"Does everybody have their boots on?"

This was a phrase I would always say just before the bell. For without this important and final item of outdoor clothing, recess could not be enjoyed or experienced at all! The students would not have been fully prepared for recess. Consequences, such as wet feet, frozen feet, sore feet, and bruised feet, could have happened.

As Christians, we can be reminded, through proper footwear, to stand our ground using the Word of God, and move forward and share the gospel of peace with others. If we don't have this piece of armour, we won't be prepared or ready for whatever lies ahead.

For shoes, put on the peace that comes from the Good News so that you will be fully prepared.

—Ephesians 6:15

Whom Are We Imitating?

Quite often, teachers tend to multitask.

On this particular day, I was consumed with assessing students, running learning centres, and managing individual needs as they arose. In a nutshell, a lot of "stuff" was going on in the classroom. Paying attention to the many interactions happening throughout the classroom was challenging.

Think about how parents might feel when they arrive home from a busy day at work, exhausted, and each family member is contributing to a conversation, not necessarily the same one, and everyone is talking at once. To add to the noise confusion, the television is turned on and it adds to the noise and projects its own message, whether good or not so good.

During play centre time on this day, a group of four boys congregated at the kitchen centre. My ears tuned in when one of the little boys said to the others, "Wanna play master chef?" I listened in on their conversation.

I wonder how this is all going to go, I thought, thinking it unusual that a five-year-old has obviously been watching an adult cooking program. The interesting thing is, they must've all been familiar with this show, as they proceeded to "imitate" the happenings of the television program. Thankfully, this television show was appropriate for children—a cooking competition program that would most likely pass the general guidance rating. This show aired years before the networks came up with the many children's cooking and baking programs now available for viewing and entertainment.

Children often imitate or reenact what they've seen or watched on television. It could be a cartoon, a commercial, or an event from the 6:00 news. The values portrayed might not have strong moral or ethical values. This can't be predicted.

What are the kids watching?

Whom are they imitating?

Imitate God, therefore, in everything you do, because you are his dear children.

—Ephesians 5:1

Story Fifteen: That Teacher Look

Who Is the Teacher?

We often get a good look at ourselves, not by looking in a mirror, but by viewing ourselves in others who may be acting like us or mimicking our behaviours.

Teachers often over-emphasize or enthusiastically communicate ideas to their students, by using their voice, actions, and facial expressions. It becomes habitual or even routine.

It was approximately 9:10 in the morning. One of my students had arrived late. The protocol for late arrival required the student to submit a late slip, which the teacher needed to fill in with pertinent information and then which the student needed to take to the office, located at the end of a long hallway, a fair distance from the kindergarten classroom.

This young student was rather timid and needed a bit of support and encouragement to make this trip. I would normally send a classmate to accompany the tardy student, but this little person refused. I quickly decided to watch him walk down the long hallway to deliver his late slip.

My classroom was slightly to the left of the hallway, so I couldn't see directly into the classroom but could hear everything quite easily. Giggles and laughter started to echo out of the classroom. *Something must be very humorous*, I thought.

The little boy made his way back down the hallway to me and we entered the classroom together.

I was startled to see two little girls sitting on my reading rocking chair, each shaking their finger at the students who were sitting on the carpet. I realized they were mimicking my actions, as well as my "You need to listen" look. They were funny, but, truth be told, it was also a reflection on how my every move was being observed, monitored, and absorbed.

I thought carefully. "Okay, Mrs. Hoff number one and Mrs. Hoff number two, it's time to sit on the carpet with your friends."

They quickly bounced of the rocker and happily joined the students on the carpet.

One day as he saw the crowds gathering, Jesus went up on the mountainside and sat down. His disciples gathered around him and he began to teach them. (Matthew 5:1–2)

Story Sixteen: Sledding Down the Hill

What Does "Follow Me" Mean?

One sunny winter day, my students and I headed out to the playground to slide down the snow-covered hill. This was the children's first go at it and everyone was excited.

We picked up the crazy carpets from the storage area and lined up at the playground doors. I gave instructions for the students to follow me. I walked them to the hill and demonstrated how to go up the hill safely. I showed them how to sit on the crazy carpet and slide down the hill. I demonstrated how to move out of the way once reaching the bottom of the hill. I showed them the importance of moving out of the way of oncoming sliders. Finally, I showed them how to climb up the side of the hill to return to the top of the hill for another slide down.

With our crazy carpets rolled up under our arms, we proceeded to the hill.

I could hear the swishing of snow pants behind me as we shuffled our way toward the hill. So far, so good! Everyone staying in line, "following" my lead. The students didn't charge past me, even when the hill was just steps away.

Up I went to the top of the hill. I noticed that the sound of the swishing snowsuits behind me had fallen silent. I turned around as I reached the top of the hill. Twenty-five little bundled-up faces stared up at me from the bottom of the hill! The hill was quite large, so all of us would have been able to stand on top together!

I don't know why, nor did I question why, they all stopped at the bottom of the hill instead of following me up to the very top. Perhaps they wanted to get a good view of how to slide down the hill, which, in all honesty, was not very graceful on my part. In any case, the students did a great job following me to the bottom of the snow hill. They just didn't follow me all the way up.

Are we following Jesus as we should? All the way? Or are we stopping at some point along our path for reasons only each of us—and God—know?

Jesus spoke to the people once more and said, "I am the light of the world. If you follow me, you won't have to walk in darkness, because you will have the light that leads to life."
—John 8:12

Jesus called out to them, "Come follow me, and I will show you how to fish for people!"

—Matthew 4:19

What Does "Follow Me" Mean?

Then Jesus said to his disciples, "If any of you wants to be my follower, you must give up your own way, take up your cross, and follow me."

—Matthew 16:24

Who Are the Bad Guys?

The big day was here—our class fieldtrip! We'd been learning about community helpers. To enrich our learning about police officers, we planned a trip to the local police station.

The students enjoyed touring through the different areas of the building, which included a fingerprinting area, office spaces, interview rooms, property rooms, lockers, a car park for the different vehicles, and, of course, cells for detainees.

The officer in charge of our tour walked us by the open and empty cells, located in the basement of the station.

Right then, one of my little students piped up. "When do we get to see the bad guys?"

I can't remember how the officer responded, but I'm sure it was with dignity and grace. I do remember my students being a little disappointed that they would not be seeing any "bad guys" on that tour.

Fieldtrips are an important part of an educational experience. They provide real-life learning opportunities. These experiences provoke further understanding and expand learning through inquiry-based learning.

Why do people go to jail?
What choices did they make that got them there?
Did they learn from their mistakes?
To whom can we turn when we make a mistake?

I want to do what is good, but I don't. I don't want to do what is wrong, but I do it anyway. But if I do what I don't want to do, I am not really the one doing wrong; it is sin living in me that does it. I have discovered this principle of life—that when I want to do what is right, I inevitably do what is wrong. I love God's law with all my heart. But there is another power within me that is at war with my mind. This power makes me a slave to the sin that is still within me. Oh what a miserable person I am! Who will free me from this life that is dominated by sin and death? Thank God! The answer is in Jesus Christ our Lord.

—Romans 7:19–25

The Bible certainly had its fair share of villains!

Did people from the Bible go to jail?

God uses the "good guys" and the "bad guys" to bring about His divine purpose and His glory!

"Don't be afraid," Samuel reassured them. "You have certainly done wrong, but make sure now that you worship the Lord with all your heart, and don't turn your back on him."
—1 Samuel 12:20

What Are You Eating?

S tory time was one of my favourite activities of the day. There are so many amazing storybooks to read.

One afternoon, I read the book, *The Hungry Thing*, by Jan Slepian. It's a fun book about a hungry creature; the author uses rhyme and phonemic awareness to engage the students in the story.

My students were enamoured with the book, which allowed them to actively participate during the story by guessing what the creature wanted to eat.

I usually planned an educational activity after story time. As I distributed sheets of paper to the students, I observed how every single little person hovered around me to receive their copy. All their little hands extended toward me. They reminded me of a nest full of baby birds, all eager to receive a portion of what the mama bird was dishing out. In a sense, they were fervent and hungry to learn.

I told them that they reminded me of the "Hungry Thing" in the book, with the sign that said "Feed Me."

A few of the students started to repeat the phrase, "Feed Me," then they all chimed in: "Feed Me, Feed Me." The chant did not stop until every student had their worksheet. As each student received their paper, they showed a sense of satisfaction. Their need was fulfilled; they quietly returned to their workspace.

Obviously, the students were not about to eat the paper. However, one could definitely say that their minds were being fed. This protocol continued each time I handed out a worksheet. I wonder what passersby were thinking when they heard us?

God feeds us. God cares for our every need.

"Look at the birds. They don't plant or harvest or store food in barns, for your heavenly Father feeds them. And aren't you far more valuable to him than they are?"

—Matthew 6:26

God also feeds us with His Word.

Yes, he humbled you by letting you go hungry and then feeding you with manna, a food previously unknown to you and your ancestors. He did it to teach you that people do not live by bread alone; rather, we live by every word that comes from the mouth of the Lord.

—Deuteronomy 8:3

Story Nineteen: Keychain

Who Is Watching You?

Teachers often wear their school keys around their necks or on their belts so they don't lose them.

I decided to try the extremely popular lanyard, first around my neck, which was not ideal, as it dangled down and knocked my students as I would bend or lean in to help them with a task. Then I decided to attach it to my belt loop around my waist, which obviously only worked if my pants had belt loops (it became a nuisance). Finally, I found a device that worked for me. I used a plastic band that stretched. I attached my keys to it and always wore it on my upper arm.

Sometimes I needed to retrieve supplies or equipment from another room. Sometimes I needed to call upon one or two mature, trustworthy, reliable students to help me out. (Remember, this is kindergarten.) There was always one student every year who qualified. The second person needed a break from the classroom and would benefit from partnering with the student who demonstrated leadership skills.

One afternoon, my class was headed outside for physical education. I needed some soccer balls and pylons from the room across the hall. I asked for two volunteers. Of course, I already knew who one of them would be.

The student I chose took my key band from me and slid the keychain up his arm. He wore the band exactly how I did. I watched in amazement. I realized that little eyes were always watching me.

Who else is watching me? Who else is watching you? The answer: God is always watching us!

The Lord is watching everywhere, keeping his eye on both the evil and the good.

—Proverbs 15:3

Why Is a Schoolteacher an Important Role Model to Others?

As a student, I remember going to elementary school and believing that whatever my teacher said was right and true and undeniable. Often, we hear this from our own children: "My teacher said!"

In high school, other voices seemed to take over, such as those of peers and various social groups, perhaps even a T.V. show character.

For some reason, as children get older, the voices of their parents, teachers, and elders fade. The voices of experience, wisdom, and love are replaced with contemporary ideas of the popular culture.

In some situations, unfortunately, many children are growing up without their parents, making it all that much more critical for teachers to hold themselves to high moral standards according to God's Word: the absolute truth.

Wow! This is such an important role. This is not an easy position, to say the least, given the present society in which we live.

One day after lunch, my kindergarten students were sitting at their tables, quietly working on an assignment. Suddenly, a little girl piped up: "Mrs. Hoff when you die, I wanna be you!"

I was taken aback, to say the least. This statement continues to amuse me; however, it also makes me wonder how little children perceive the role models who are present in their lives.

"Do you mean that you want to be a kindergarten teacher?" I asked.

"NO! I wanna be *you*!" she replied adamantly.

I must have made kindergarten and my role/position look extremely appealing. So wonderful, in fact, that in her eyes, she would rather be me than herself.

> *"Students are not greater than their teacher. But the student who is fully trained will become like the teacher."*
>
> —Luke 6:40

God has a special purpose for each one of us. If we want to be like someone, Jesus is our ultimate role model.

> *Come and listen to my counsel. I'll share my heart with you and make you wise.*
>
> —Proverbs 1:23

> *Don't copy the behaviour and customs of this world, but let God transform you into a new person by changing the way*

you think. Then you will learn to know God's will for you, which is good and pleasing and perfect.

—Romans 12:2

The following is a verse that would apply to teachers of the Bible, pastors, church elders, leaders, Sunday school teachers, and all who have been called to teach the word:

Dear brothers and sisters, not many of you should become teachers in the church, for we who teach will be judged more strictly.
—James 3:1

Schoolteachers should also pay heed to this verse.

Whom Are We Listening To?

Listening to the voice of someone in authority is something we're all trained to do. Students need to listen to the teacher and obey the instructions the teacher gives. What happens if the students refuse or perhaps listen to someone other than the teacher in charge? Consequences!

One such incident occurred in my classroom just before morning recess. The students were busy finishing up their snack and tidying their spot. At this point, I walked over to the classroom door and called the students to line up when they were ready. This meant that personal items were put away and they were sitting quietly.

A student in my class, a little boy, slight of stature, who was just learning to speak English, absolutely loved recess. When he spoke, it was with a noticeable accent. He happily followed along with class procedures.

Before snack, we'd been colouring with markers. This little guy had a bit of black marker under his nose, likely because he must have been itchy and scratched above his lip with fresh marker from his finger.

He must've been extremely excited to go outside for recess. Once he saw me walk over to the classroom door, he jumped up and bolted ahead of me. Out of his mouth came two words very clearly, very loudly, and with ultimate authority: "LINE UP!"

Simultaneously, this small child lifted his arm high in the air, a body signal used school-wide to silence the room. Every single student dropped what they were doing and immediately obeyed the command and proceeded to line up. I watched in amazement as the students formed their recess line. I smiled and calmly reminded them that they needed to listen for my voice as the signal that we were all set to go. Then I asked them to take their seats and finish what they were doing.

This was a mild case of hearing and doing something that did not come from the official voice of authority. The situation was quickly remedied and brought under the command of myself.

So, whom are we listening to? God is sovereign. God has supreme authority. God is in control. If we listen to God, through His Word, we clearly hear His voice and instruction.

Those who listen to instruction will prosper; those who trust the Lord will be joyful.

—Proverbs 16:20

If you fully obey the Lord your God and carefully keep all his commands that I am giving you today, the Lord your God will set you high above all the nations of the world. You will experience all these blessings if you obey the Lord your God.

—Deuteronomy 28: 1–2

What Is a Tall Tale?

Tall tales are usually exaggerations of actual events or stories. Show-and-tell was a time for students to bring an item from home to show others, talk about it, and answer questions. If a student forgot or didn't have an item to show, they were welcomed to *tell* the class something instead.

Students were always eager to share, in detail, personal family life experiences with others. Often, if a student was unsure of what to share, they would expand upon what another student shared. They would fit it into their own personal or family version.

During one of our show-and-tell sessions, a student asked to use the washroom. When he returned to the group, he informed me that he was afraid to flush the toilet because it might flood. Apparently, he experienced this at home the night before. Seconds later, a little hand shot up into the air. A little boy with wide eyes and excitement in his voice began to tell his own version of this incident.

"That happened to me. I flushed and the water came up out of the toilet and flooded the bathroom. The water went out of the bathroom and filled the house. I had to put on a life jacket. My dad opened the door and I floated right out!"

I'm hoping he was just floating in toilet water!

Truthful words stand the test of time, but lies are soon exposed.
—Proverbs 12:19

What Can Affect Hearing?

Routines in kindergarten classrooms are essential for an organized, stable environment. In September, students learn and practice routines specific to their grade level. By October, students need to be on board and ready to learn.

Upon entering the classroom, students would find their name card at a table and place it in a pocket chart. Then they would return to their seat at the table and engage in a semi-quiet table activity until all members of the class had arrived and attendance was taken.

Next, a VIP (Very Important Person), was selected through a lottery turn-taking process. A fun title I picked up from my own children's kindergarten teacher, the VIP was the student leader for the day and had many important and vital leadership roles and tasks.

The very first job of the day was to lead classmates in a movement activity. VIPs would position themselves in front of the classroom. Students were asked to stand behind their chairs and move through a series of actions while repeating a word chant. (Note: I picked up the chant from observing my own kid's swimming lesson. The swim instructor used it to motivate the children to jump into the swimming pool.) I modified it and used it to get my students to engage, wiggle the jiggles out, and provide an opportunity for social participation.

The first line of the chant goes like this: "Bananas Unite!" (simultaneously, both arms were raised above the head with hands clapped together above the head). The VIP waited for all classmates to copy this action and freeze in this position. The chant continued with specific words and actions for the students to copy. The activity ended with the students being instructed to sit down.

We had been participating in this activity for about a month. The current VIP for the day was the last person to receive a turn; by now, the chant had become routine. Students knew the words and actions.

This young boy who was leading the class began: "Bananas Tonight!"

Woops! What was that?

"Bananas Tonight!" repeated the students. I smiled and held back the instinctive laugh that was bubbling inside me. All this time, this boy was hearing "Bananas Tonight," yet continuing to bring his arms up together in the unified action. The word "tonight" must have made more sense to him. Bananas would be on the evening menu!

How easy it is to mishear something so simple.

Then he added, "Pay close attention to what you hear. The closer you listen, the more understanding you will be given—and you will receive even more."
—Mark 4:24

Let's think a little deeper. Are we truly listening and hearing to what God is saying? What is affecting what we hear? Possibly our own will? Maybe unintentional misunderstanding? Perhaps we are just not paying attention!

But don't just listen to God's word. You must do what it says.
—James 1:22a

Story Twenty-Four: You Look Like the Mayor!

How Do Others See You?

Teachers are often required to adhere to a "professional" dress code. Dress-down days are provided with a good cause or purpose that encourages participation.

A school I worked at for most of my career set aside every Friday for staff to dress down (basically, this means staff are permitted to wear jeans). A small monetary donation was required to participate; the funds went to charities agreed upon by the participants.

That left four out of five days to plan clothes/outfits for the specified manner of dress at school. I enjoyed fashion; however, it did provide challenges for me as a kindergarten teacher. Choosing items that were washable, stain-resistant, and comfortable proved to be an exigent task.

One day, upon returning home from a typical day teaching, my daughter asked, "What happened to you?"

I was somewhat taken aback with her words. However, after glancing over myself and peering into the front hallway mirror, I realized I was wearing bits of my day. White paint and wool strands were stuck in my hair from the craft we made, and speckles of mud dotted my pants from my knees to my ankles from recess supervision.

My daughter perceived my physical appearance as though I had encountered a hapless situation. I shrugged my shoulders, as this was an everyday side-effect of my job.

A similar, but opposite perception of my appearance took place at school. Apparently, my clothing attire choice sparked the attention of one of my students. Dressed in a pair of black pants, white blouse, black vest, and black pumps, I entered the classroom. I walked over to the carpeted morning meeting area where the students were waiting for me.

"You look like the mayor!" one boy blurted out.

Wow, what an impression I must have made!

How does God see us?

The Lord doesn't see things the way you see them. People judge by outward appearance, but the Lord looks at the heart.
—1 Samuel 16:7b

Since God chose you to be the holy people he loves, you must clothe yourselves with tenderhearted mercy, kindness, humility, gentleness, and patience.

—Colossians 3:12

Story Twenty-Five: Don't Use This Finger!

What Is Conveyed by a Gesture?

It was the very first day of kindergarten. A fresh start to a brand-new year. So exciting! Oh, the wonderful things we would all learn together.

Who would have thought that a group of six students would go home that day showing their parents and caregivers how to use one of their fingers as a bad word?

The first day of school is often very overwhelming for students and teachers alike, filled with joy and laughter, excitement and curiosity, tears and fears, and many hugs and kisses from moms and dads to their children.

I usually stood inside the classroom close to the door greeting each new face and directing the student to a table that had a personal name card indicating their seating place for the day. Six students were designated to each table. Some tables filled up sooner than others.

On this particular morning, a group of students at one of the tables was making soft "oohing" sounds. I was speaking with a parent at the door, but out of the corner of my eye, I observed that one little girl seemed to have the attention of every single person at the table.

As soon as I had finished my conversation, I curiously moved toward the "oohing" table. Five little faces looked up at me, puzzled and shocked. I knew this would be an "oh dear" moment!

The girl leading the conversation looked at me in a very matter-of-fact way and simultaneously spoke and waved a gesture at me and her tablemates. Her little middle finger popped up and she began waving it in the air.

"You aren't supposed to use this finger; it's a bad word. It means the 'f' word, right, Mrs. Hoff?"

"Mrs. Hoff, What's the 'f' word?" another student asked.

Oh dear indeed! This was certainly not how I would have preferred the start of the very first day of school to go, and certainly not the form of communication that's acceptable.

Thankfully, the public school I was teaching at had not yet removed the Lord's Prayer, which was recited every morning before announcements. I quickly asked all students to copy my "praying hands" and "head-bowing" gestures.

The intercom voice echoed through the speaker: "Would you please bow your heads for the Lord's Prayer?" After the prayer, I firmly and gently explained to my brand-new students that we needed to focus on what we should be doing, rather than what we're not supposed to do. Later, during circle time, we discussed school and classroom rules. My number-one rule was: "Hands are for helping, not hurting."

What Is Conveyed by a Gesture?

Make it your goal to live a quiet life, minding your own business and working with your hands, just as we instructed you before

—1 Thessalonians 4:11

Story Twenty-Six: Little Lamb

Who Is Mary?

It was the Christmas season, with upcoming celebrations and activities focused around the birthday of Jesus Christ.

Before reading or introducing any storybook, I always posed a pre-story question.

My question on that December afternoon was, "Who is Mary?"

As expected, every little hand was raised high in the air. Eager, almost exploding little bodies spasmed with enthusiasm. I quickly chose a student to give their answer.

"Mary Had a Little Lamb!" exclaimed a little girl with a confident voice.

"Yes, she did."

Immediately, most of the little hands returned to their laps. Not quite the answer I was looking for; however, I could make it work. You might have been expecting the answer that I was: Mary is Jesus's mother.

Many seasonal worship songs emphasize this. There's another little tune, a nursery rhyme that most children are familiar with. The first line of the first verse is: "Mary had a little lamb" and the last line of the first verse is, "its fleece was white as snow."

Jesus is referred to as the "Lamb of God." Jesus was sacrificed to take away our sins.

> *The next day John saw Jesus coming toward him and said, "Look! The Lamb of God who takes away the sin of the world!"*

—John 1:29

When we repent, we are made clean, as white as snow.

> *"Come now, let's settle this," says the Lord. "Though your sins are like scarlet, I will make them as white as snow. Though they are red like crimson, I will make them as white as wool."*

—Isaiah 1:18

God chose Mary to be Jesus's mother. Mary gave birth to Jesus. Hence, "Mary had a little Lamb."

> *Mary asked the angel, "But how can this happen? I am a virgin." The angel replied, "The Holy Spirit will come upon you, and the power of the Most High will overshadow you. So the baby to be born will be holy, and he will be called the Son of God."*

—Luke 1:34–35

What Will It Cost?

K indergarten classes in the school divisions I worked for were scheduled half time for the year. Students attended full days, every second day.

Yet the children were always commenting that they "wished they could come to school every day!"

To help students understand the timeframe of attending school every other day, I would often engage in instructional conversation to emphasize today and tomorrow.

A phrase I used to effectively strengthen this understanding was: "Free today, twenty-five dollars tomorrow." I repeated this to every student as they received their pencil and paper assignment. The students would actively engage by pretending to pay me different amounts of money, such as fifty dollars, one hundred dollars, one thousand dollars, usually trying to outdo their classmates. They were willing to pay very generous amounts for one single sheet of paper, even though I always repeated the words, "Free today!"

I also reminded them that they would not be at school tomorrow. The students insisted on trying to pay me or "buy" the free gift I was offering them—most likely because they were having fun with this idea.

However, Jesus also offers us a free gift today. He paid for our sin so that we might receive the gift of eternal life. It can be very costly not to accept God's free gift today. Tomorrow could be too late!

> *For the wages of sin is death, but the free gift of God is eternal life through Christ Jesus our Lord.*
>
> —Romans 6:23

> *For God bought you with a high price. So you must honor God with your body.*
>
> —1 Corinthians 6:20

What Is a Copycat?

I have asked my students to copy me on many occasions for a variety of reasons—one is to get their attention.

It's always a good idea to discuss what's appropriate to copy and what isn't. I used fun learning activities to promote the right kind of copying. A well-known game, Simon Says, is perfect for this. We read a variety of storybooks that focused on good and not-so-good copying. Musical instruments also worked well. Students took turns leading classmates in a rhythm pattern or sound patterns to copy.

My personal favourite "copy me" attention-grabber is a quick clapping rhythm common to most educators. It goes, clap-clap, clap-clap-clap. Sometimes, the students can become accustomed to the same cue if it's repeated too many times, and therefore tune out. I found it beneficial to mix it up a bit. I would clap different rhythms, add my voice by singing a familiar line of a song, or add a series of hand-and-body movements. The students had to pay attention to copy me exactly. All eyes watching, all ears listening, all actions and sounds repeated in unison. This signaled to me that we were ready to move forward with instruction.

One morning, I was leading the class in a series of "copy me" actions. I must have been experiencing a bit of brain fog. I seemed to be struggling to come up with the actions for the students to copy. I tilted my head up to think. My mind was blank; however, my fingers inadvertently started to quickly wiggle by my sides as my brain pondered what to do next.

After about ten seconds, I glanced at my students and noticed that every single one of them was wiggling their fingers by their side.

Why are they all doing that? I wondered.

Then I looked at my own hands and started to laugh. Wouldn't you know it, the students all started to laugh too! I smiled; they smiled! They really took it to heart when I asked them to copy me. Of course, one student asked me, "What was so funny, Mrs. Hoff?"

Whom are we copying and why? This is what the Bible instructs:

> *Don't copy the behaviour and customs of this world, but let God transform you into a new person by changing the way you think. Then you will learn to know God's will for you, which is good and pleasing and perfect.*
>
> —Romans 12:2

Story Twenty-Nine: I'm Done!

Are You Overwhelmed?

One morning, my class was working on a reading rebus poem. We had read the poem together as a group. Now it was time for the students to work independently at their table. First, I instructed them to colour the pictures in the poem. Next, they needed to use their pointer finger to track and read the words and pictures from left to right, using a quiet whispering voice.

The students diligently began working on the task at hand. The room was as quiet as a church mouse.

Suddenly, a booming voice resounded from one of the tables. "I'm done!"

I looked over at the student and observed that in a matter of the few minutes after beginning the task, that he had used his crayons to colour over the entire page. I glanced at the other students who were carefully colouring each rebus picture.

Obviously, this young boy had hurried through his work. Sometimes I request students to redo a task if I think they've rushed through the assignment. In this situation, I asked the student to please read the poem if he was done colouring. The young boy turned in his seat and complied.

Fewer than ten seconds had passed, and once again, the same voice, in a loud and obtrusive manner, declared, "I'm done!" I looked over and said, "Read it again." The student looked at me for a few seconds and then complied. Within moments of his previous outburst, he proceeded to proclaim he was done, once again.

I was occupied with helping another student properly hold their crayon. So, I looked up and over at the boy and said, "Read it ten times!"

"Ten times? Oh my G——!" he cried out in distress.

I was startled by his choice of words; they caught me by surprise! After this outburst, I quickly realized that he was overwhelmed.

"Okay, tidy your spot and choose a learning centre to work and play at," I replied.

He jumped up quickly and quietly from his chair, deposited his pencil box and poem into their designated places for storage, and made his way to the choice chart. With an expression of relief, he happily engaged in building a bridge with the wooden blocks.

All the while, the remainder of the students continued to focus on the assigned task. Honestly, I did not expect him to read the poem ten times. When we ask our students to do their best work, the realization of what that means and how students go about it will vary with each individual.

The next time we engaged in the same type of academic task, I very specifically guided him by breaking down the assignment into bite-sized portions. This resulted in his best work, and only a one-time response of, "I'm done!"

For I can do everything through Christ, who gives me strength.
—Philippians 4:13

Story Thirty: I Like Your Outfit!

Whom Should We Look Like?

School-wide social activities are intermittently planned by student leadership groups to promote school spirit and comradery. Fun and uplifting events take place to celebrate being part of a community, as well as to promote friendship in positive ways.

Spirit week was in full swing within our school. With many to-do tasks occupying my mind, I sometimes forgot what the theme of the day was. Kudos to the students' parents who well prepared their children for these special celebratory days!

One morning, a student of mine walked into the classroom with a big smile on her face. I immediately noticed how fashionable she looked. I smiled back at her. "I like your outfit!"

She started to giggle and pointed at me. I was confused. Then she pointed at my tall black knee boots, and then to her own black boots. Now the gears in my brain were clicking. She then pointed to her long sweater; interesting, as I, too, was wearing a long sweater. Next, she pointed to her knee-length pencil skirt. Of course, I was also wearing a knee-length pencil skirt.

Finally, she pointed to her blouse that she wore slightly over the waist of her skirt. I nodded as we finished this pointing game.

"It's Dress-Up-Like-a-Teacher Day, isn't it?" I said to break the silence.

We both laughed. What a precious, sweet, and genuine compliment I received from this little girl.

Whom are we supposed to resemble?

Dear friends, we are already God's children, but he has not yet shown us what we will be like when Christ appears. But we do know that we will be like him, for we will see him as he really is.

—1 John 3:2

Story Thirty-One: Magnifying Glasses and the Human Chain Link: Lost but Now Found!

What Are You Looking For?

S cience class—an opportunity to use cool equipment and study nature at the same time!

The warm spring air was an inviting call to take science class outdoors. Our unit of study was bugs. Perfect! Warm weather in the month of May, in Saskatchewan, is an opportune time and excellent breeding ground for a variety of insects.

My class had used magnifying glasses earlier in the school year, so I was confident that they knew how to properly use them. My one concern was that there was a possibility of losing one or two of them in the vastness of the playground field.

Off we went. Students in groups of three, each group member responsible for one item. The first member was in charge of the magnifying glass, the second of the butterfly bug net, and the third of the plastic bug jar.

I signalled to the students to let them know that it was time to trade science tools within their group by blowing a whistle.

The students were spread out over the school grounds, frantically running about, chasing the bugs in the air. Others were bent over bushes or crawling in the grass, seeking out creepy crawlies.

After about thirty minutes, I observed a few students tumbling on top of each other, indicating they were done and had had enough of bug hunting for the day.

I gathered them all together to go back to the classroom, first checking that each group member had the item for which they were responsible. Upon doing a student head count and equipment check, I had confirmation that all students were accounted for and that one magnifying glass was, in fact, missing in action. What to do? I could look for the magnifying glass on my own, later after school, or produce quicker results through a group effort.

There is a saying, "Many hands make light work" (John Heywood), so how about many eyes as well?

I quickly lined the students up, side by side, forming a human chain link. We linked arms and took a step forward, searching the ground for the magnifying glass. After about ten steps forward, one of my students yelled out, "Found it!"

Lo and behold, the missing magnifying glass was recovered!

Parable of the Lost Coin:

Or suppose a woman has ten silver coins and loses one. Won't she light a lamp and sweep the entire house and search carefully until she finds it? In the same way, there is joy in the presence of God's angels when even one sinner repents.

—Luke 15:8 &10

What Are You Looking For?

For the Son of Man came to seek and save those who are lost.
—Luke 19:10

Do We Listen and Respond When We Are Called?

Often, it takes more than one request by the teacher for students to listen and comply to the teacher's direction. Once the students become familiar with classroom routines and procedures, listening improves immensely!

One young lad whom I remember fondly really struggled with learning to listen and listening to learn. I put into practice many behavioural strategies to help this student in this area of development. I would call upon this boy by name over and over again to gain his attention. I would sing his name. I would use positive praise, offer choices, the list goes on. The option to give up does not exist. A teacher keeps trying until a solution is discovered. After all, we want the best for our students.

The 9:00 a.m. bell rang. The students made their way into the school in their usual cheerful, clamorous manner. Students congregated at the lockers removing outerwear clothing. One by one, they entered the classroom.

The usual, "Hi, Mrs. Hoff!" was echoed with each arrival, except for one—my young friend with listening challenges.

Abruptly, and with authority, he announced, "Mrs. Hoff, I'm not Marcus anymore; I'm Voltar!"

I looked at him and responded, "Good morning, Voltar. Please sit down and be quiet."

This time, he responded very quickly to my command. When I used his pretend name, he obeyed and listened to my direction on the first request. Finally, a strategy that worked! Who would have thought?

Do you think God tries to get our attention over and over again, but we fail to hear our name being called? Do we listen to Him and obey Him the first time He summons us?

> *Then he took the Book of the Covenant and read it aloud to the people. Again they all responded, "We will do everything the Lord has commanded. We will obey."*
>
> —Exodus 24:7

Story Thirty-Three: An Emergency!

Can We Save Someone?

Community helpers was our next unit of study—one of my favourites!

I asked my students a general question to begin the thought process: "Are there people who can help or save others?" and "Who are they, or what do they do?"

The students were well versed on the topic. Many of their parents worked in positions or had careers that would be considered a helping job. Responses flowed. Firefighter, police officer, nurse, doctor, dentist, tow truck driver, bus driver, teacher, farmer and more! Essentially, all responses were accepted. We could confirm that every job had its own unique helping qualities. After all, our number-one class rule was "Hands are for helping, not hurting!"

We were a very blessed class and school, as many of the parents volunteered to visit the classroom and share their job with us, often bringing specialized equipment they used and their source of transportation that coincided if possible. An array of police and RCMP cars, firetrucks, paramedic vehicles, construction trucks, school busses, and more pulled into the parking lot at the front of the school. We would know the exact time of their arrival as our east school wall faced the parking lot and the window extended the entire length of the classroom from north to south. The thrilling squeals from the students foretold of the excitement to follow, as we learned about community helpers as well as welcomed our special parent guests! Hands-on learning in the most meaningful way.

This year at school was also a particularly difficult one for me. My healthy and active mom became unexpectantly ill. Frequently, I was called away from school to attend medical appointments and tend to family concerns, as needed. It was a battle that took my family up and down hills. It left us spending a great deal of time in the valley of uncertainty and, for my mom, the valley of sickness and suffering.

Guest teachers were common in my classroom. I usually prepared my students for my absence. Christmas came and went that year. It was heartbreaking, as I knew my mom's health condition was deteriorating quickly. We spent Christmas break at the hospital in the palliative care unit with my mom and immediate family. We gathered to comfort and cherish these final days of my mom's life. Hope never left our hearts. Our mom, grandmother to our children, wife of more than 50 years to our dad was cognoscente up until her last day. It was hard to let her go. She served others, was extremely active in her church community, and loved the Lord with all her heart. She loved to laugh and enjoy fellowship with others. She was full of energy and vitality. She, who had always looked fifteen years younger than her biological age, became hardly recognizable on the outside. On the inside, her being was still strong as she would try to squeeze our hands to let us know she was our loving mother.

We prayed.

On January sixth, I returned to class to prepare for a longer-term guest teacher and explain to my students that I would be away for awhile. My mom, being the fighter that she was, continued her battle for one more day; her resilience for life was extraordinary.

By mid-morning on that day, I received a call at school to go directly to the hospital. It was bitter cold. The intercom in the classroom messaged the staff and students that recess would be spent indoors. I put a movie on for the students to watch and told them I had an emergency and had to leave right away.

A little boy looked up at me. "Mrs. Hoff, are you going to save somebody?"

"No; only God can save us," I replied, looking down at his eyes gazing up at me.

My mom went to be with the Lord on the next day, January seventh—her Ukrainian Christmas.

For God loved the world so much that he gave his one and only Son, so that everyone who believes in him will not perish but have eternal life.

—John 3:16

Story Thirty-Four: The Writing on the Wall

Where Did You Get the Chalk From?

"The writing on the wall" is a well-known phrase that you've probably heard before. It indicates that a situation might result in an unpleasant consequence.

The two stories I will share are similar in content. The first occurred at the start of my career as a parent; the second, as a teacher in my final (retirement) year.

Part One

Reading and signing a child's agenda book daily is one form or tool of communication used between teachers, parents, and students.

I pulled out my oldest child's agenda from his backpack, realizing I hadn't seen it for a couple of days—odd, but life happens. The agenda appeared to be stuffed to the bottom of the backpack under a pile of non-essential items, burying the agenda completely. I pulled it out and proceeded to sign the page for the current date.

Then I looked back at what I might have missed over the last couple of days. My heart sank and I could feel my face heating up with frustration. I immediately figured out why my second-grade child had been keeping his agenda from both his mother's and father's eyes.

A note from his teacher informed us that an incident had occurred at school. Apparently, over afternoon recess a few days ago prior, my son and his friend were writing on the outdoor brick wall of the school with chalk. They were discovered because they had written their names beside their lovely drawings. Both boys had to wash the school wall and lost recess privileges for a day—what I thought was a reasonable consequence for the innocent, yet intentional, graffiti.

I wrote back in the agenda, expressing my sincere apologies for not responding immediately to the note in the agenda. My husband and I had a chat with our child about hiding the agenda from us, which was the more serious concern in the situation. One of the curious questions on my mind was,

"Where did you get the chalk from?" we asked him.

The answer? From the other boy's mom's classroom; she was the kindergarten teacher at the school!

Part Two

It was common in my class for students to use sports equipment and various items of novelty to occupy their recess productively.

My students needed an outdoor, fresh air "brain break." It was a sunny, warm spring day, so off we went for a fifteen-minute recess. I gave the students two activity options: They could either play on the climbing structure or draw with sidewalk chalk on the pavement.

Four students chose the chalk. I showed them where they could use it. A patch of uneven, rough ground surface was the space available. Next, I walked toward the play structure to check on the other students—about fifty feet away straight north of the "chalk group," which was in full view.

As expected, a couple of students who were playing on the structure had a small kerfuffle that needed my attention. It took only a few moments to solve the minor dispute. Then I looked over to see what the chalk group was up to. I couldn't believe my eyes! The four students—two boys and two girls—were all drawing on the side of the school wall. By the time I was in ear shot range of the students, quite a large area of the wall was decorated with their creative artwork and, of course, their names!

I called to the students to stop. They looked over at me and waited until I arrived on scene.

"Why are you writing on the school wall?" They could sense I was a bit upset. "It's smoother than the ground," one of the girls answered simply.

Off we all went—the entire class—to get some buckets of water and sponges to wash the wall and clean off the chalk. As we walked by the Grade Four class, with buckets of water in hand, the teacher and her students were wondering what fun and interesting activity we were doing now. When she asked me this later, I laughed and explained the situation.

The answer to the story title question, "Where did you get the chalk from?", is, again "the kindergarten teacher!"

In a rather unique way, these two stories reflect that what goes around comes around, in a rather amusing and mild way, compared to the actual events that occurred in the Old Testament in Daniel 5:1–31.

> *Suddenly, they saw the fingers of a human hand writing on the plaster wall of the king's palace, near the lampstand. The king himself saw the hand as it wrote.*

—Daniel 5:5

What Is Crossfire?

October had arrived; Thanksgiving was around the corner. I had planned a traditional turkey craft for the students to make, commemorating the upcoming feast and celebration.

The first stage consisted of painting paper plates the colour brown. Every white space needed to be covered. This would be the turkey body. Supplies were all set out and distributed among the tables: a paintbrush and paper plate for every student; two containers of brown paint to share between six students at a table; three students on each side. Next, I would need to plan strategic seating. This means thoughtful planning would go into who sat beside whom, in order to make it through the first stage of the craft without too many collateral paint accidents.

The students pulled their paint shirts over their clothing and were called to a designated table to begin the project. I was satisfied that there was a good balance of students who were on-task role models, that would be able to provide leadership and responsible behaviour to those who may need someone to copy if they became an off-task painter.

I began circulating around the tables, lending a hand or positively praising students for being such amazing Picassos. Everything appeared to be going well. Then, as I approached one of the tables, I noticed that a little girl had some paint that stretched across the top of her glasses. I asked her what happened, but she quietly just shrugged her shoulders, so I let it go. This is a good time to mention that to the left and right of this little girl sat two of my more mischievous little boys. However, both seemed to be painting away, quite contently.

Clean-up went smoothly. The paper plates were set to dry, and the students washed up. Part two of the craft would continue into our next day of school: decorating the turkey with feathers and other turkey body parts.

The next morning, I chatted with the mom of the little girl who had paint across the top of her glasses. The girl's mom commented that her girls really enjoy painting. She had twin girls in my class that year. Both little girls were quiet students who were often my choice for others to copy for appropriate behaviour.

During our conversation, I commented that it was unclear how brown paint ended up smeared across the top of the girl's glasses. She had been somewhat tight-lipped about it, so we had just wiped off the paint with a tissue and carried on with painting. The mom smiled and told me that the two little boys on either side of her had had a paintbrush fight. This little girl sitting in between them was innocently caught in the crossfire.

It was not a total surprise to me, but I was a little displeased with the two boys. My strategic seating had backfired;

however, I could visualize and understand how this paint battle went down.

The Lord himself will fight for you. Just stay calm.
—Exodus 14:14

The twin sisters were brought to mind on two separate occasions over the many years that have passed since that particular kindergarten year.

The first occurred when my mom was admitted to the hospital's palliative care unit in December 2013. The mother of the twin girls was one of the attending nurses! I asked how the girls were doing and she informed me that they both were doing very well.

The second time was in April 2020, when one of the girls—now a young woman—was highlighted on the local news for sewing masks to donate during the COVID-19 pandemic.

Conclusion

In looking back at class photos of my students of days, months, and years gone by, memories flash across my mind, and the realization of how time flies sinks into a depth never understood before.

Monday and Friday both come and go with a blur. Colleagues would often give a happy shoutout: "Have a nice weekend!" to which I would reply, "Don't blink!"

If I were to have a moment to talk with former students whom I've taught over my career, I'm sure each one would have their own special memories and stories of life during their kindergarten year. I've written about only a few in this book. I'm very sure some unique and interesting situations occurred, ones of which I'm unaware. Everyone has their own memories.

Teachers don't have eyes in the back of their head. Teachers are, however, sensitive to and can perceive shifts in mood. This heightened sense alerts the educator that something is up, or about to break forth. I might not have known about every single circumstance, but life in kindergarten most definitely kept me on my toes.

On a T.V. program, I once heard author and speaker Joyce Meyer say, "Sometimes you have to put your foot in, the waters didn't part until the Israelites put their foot in."

Try to see the world from a five-year-old's eyes. The Bible reveals, through Jesus's words:

> *Then he said, "I tell you the truth, unless you turn from your sins and become like little children, you will never get into the Kingdom of Heaven. So anyone who becomes as humble as this little child is the greatest in the Kingdom of Heaven."*
>
> —Matthew 18:3–4

About the Author

Tana Hoff and her husband of thirty-three years, Michael, live in Regina, Saskatchewan, with their Husky mix dog, Stormy. They have two grown children who live in Manitoba. Tana, a retired educator of more than thirty years, is the sole proprietor of Good Life Music, a music business founded on her passion for and love of sharing music with others. Spring, summer and fall seasons are spent at their peaceful cottage in Sun Valley Resort, Saskatchewan.

Stories from Kindergarten is Tana's first book. Tana's hope is for others to know Jesus in their own personal way and to listen for and hear the music in everyday life.

www.ingramcontent.com/pod-product-compliance
Lightning Source LLC
Chambersburg PA
CBHW051430090426
42737CB00014B/2904